W9-AOV-486

Paws
AND
Claws

RED PANDAS

Sara Swan Miller

PowerKiDS
press.

New York

For Erin and Pete
Your favorites!

Published in 2008 by The Rosen Publishing Group, Inc.
29 East 21st Street, New York, NY 10010

Copyright © 2008 by The Rosen Publishing Group, Inc.

All rights reserved. No part of this book may be reproduced in any form without permission in writing from the publisher, except by a reviewer.

First Edition

Editor: Amelie von Zumbusch
Book Design: Julio Gil
Photo Researcher: Nicole Pristash

Photo Credits: Cover, pp. 7, 9, 13, 17 Shutterstock.com; p. 5 © istockphoto.com/Valerie Crafter; p. 11 © istockphoto.com/Gerard Mass; p. 15 © istockphoto.com/Ian Jeffery; p. 19 © R. Usher/Peter Arnold Inc.; p. 21 © Getty Images.

Library of Congress Cataloging-in-Publication Data

Miller, Sara Swan.
  Red pandas / Sara Swan Miller. — 1st ed.
     p. cm. — (Paws and claws)
  Includes index.
  ISBN 978-1-4042-4164-0 (library binding)
  1. Red panda—Juvenile literature. I. Title.
  QL737.C214M55 2008
  599.76'3—dc22

                                        2007020821

Manufactured in the United States of America

Contents

What Are Red Pandas?

When you think of pandas, you likely think of the well-known black and white giant pandas. Red pandas are very different and much smaller. Giant pandas are in the same family as bears. However, red pandas are grouped in a family of their own. The chief thing that giant pandas and red pandas have in common is that they both eat **bamboo**.

Red pandas live in parts of China, Nepal, India, and a few other countries in Asia. They always live in forests where bamboo grows. Most red pandas live in the mountains.

Red pandas are about the size of a large house cat. They generally weigh
between 7 and 14 pounds (3–6 kg).

Cute and Furry

Most people agree that red pandas are very cute. They have black, beady eyes and a black nose. Their pointed ears stand straight up. **Patches** on their face make red pandas look a bit like raccoons. Red pandas have a long, bushy tail that is a little like a raccoon's tail, too. A red panda's tail has yellow and reddish rings around it. Red pandas also have thick reddish coats that make them hard to see against the reddish tree branches where they often hide.

Red pandas have strong jaws, or mouths, and sharp teeth. These are perfect for tearing up bamboo shoots.

Red pandas have soft, thick coats. These coats help the pandas stay warm in their cool forest homes.

Wonderful Paws and Claws

A red panda's paws are well suited for the life it leads. They are furry, with a thick **sole**, which keeps the panda's feet warm in the snow and ice. A red panda's feet point in. This makes it easier for the panda to walk along tree branches.

A red panda has long, sharp claws that help it hold on when it climbs around in the trees. Red pandas can pull their claws partway back into their paws. That makes it easier to walk on the ground. Red pandas also have a "false thumb," which is really part of their **wrist** bone.

Check Out Receipt

Parkville-Carney Branch
410-887-5353
www.bcpl.info

Monday, June 24, 2024 11:16:53
AM
78921

Item: 31183132280097
Title: BCPL checkout item.
Call no.:
Due: 7/15/2024

Total items: 1

You just saved $35.00 by using
your library today.

Kids can register for
Summer Reading Challenge.
Get a free book and win prizes!
Ask branch staff for details.

Each of a red panda's four paws has five sharp claws.

Hungry Pandas

A red panda's false thumb helps it hold its food. Red pandas use their paws to stuff their food into their mouth. These pandas even have a special way of drinking. They stick a paw into a pool of water and then lick the water off.

Red pandas search for food at night, both on the ground and in the trees. They eat mostly bamboo, and they need a lot of it. Now and then, they will eat roots, grass, or fruit. In zoos, red pandas may be fed not only bamboo, but also **biscuits**, apples, melons, and vegetables.

Red pandas eat a lot of bamboo. Each red panda eats thousands of bamboo leaves every day.

A Quiet Life

Bamboo does not have many **calories**, so red pandas do not have much **energy**. These pandas spend most of the day sleeping. Sometimes they lie down on a branch. Other times they curl up in a hole in a tree with their furry tail curled over their face. In the evening, they finally climb down to the ground. Red pandas are wonderful climbers. Sometimes they climb down headfirst, holding on with their strong claws.

Red pandas are not very loud. Sometimes they make little twittering or **whistling** noises. Most of the time, though, they are quiet and shy.

Red pandas are nocturnal. This means they generally sleep during the day and eat at night.

Watch Out, Pandas!

Even though they lead quiet lives, red pandas do have to watch out for enemies. Martens, which are a kind of weasel, are great tree climbers themselves. Martens love to eat red pandas. Red pandas also have to watch out for snow leopards. These are big cats with very sharp teeth and claws.

Red pandas often lie still in the branches, hoping their enemies will not notice them. If a panda is cornered, it will rise up on its back legs and hiss and **grunt**. Then it strikes out with its very sharp claws.

Snow leopards live in the mountains of Asia. Snow leopards hunt red pandas, mountain sheep, wild pigs, and other animals.

Stay Out!

Red pandas spend most of their time alone. Adult pandas meet only to **mate**. Each panda has its own area, or space, where it feeds and sleeps. This area is called its territory. A red panda's territory is small, but it does not want to share it with anybody.

Every evening, a red panda travels around the edge of its territory. Red pandas have **musk glands** under their tail that give off a strong smell. The panda sprays the musk on rocks and trees all around the edge of its territory. The smell tells other pandas to go away.

A red panda's territory is fairly small. Panda territories are generally
1 to 2 square miles (3–5 sq km).

Baby Red Pandas

Just before her babies are born, a mother red panda will make a den in a hole in a tree. She lines this den with grass and leaves. Newborn red pandas are about the size of kittens. Their eyes and ears are closed, and their fur is gray. Their eyes and ears open after 18 days. Throughout this time, the mother nurses and cares for the babies.

After about two months, the babies start chasing and playing with each other. At about 70 days, their fur turns red. Finally, when the babies are three months old, they start eating bamboo.

Red panda mothers take good care of their young. This mother panda is moving her baby to a safe new hiding spot.

Disappearing Red Pandas

Red pandas are very rare, or uncommon. They are becoming even rarer. In the wild, there are fewer than 2,500 red pandas left.

People have cut down the forests where pandas used to live. People did this because they needed wood to cook and to build houses. Now the forests are farmland, with no bamboo for pandas to eat. People also let their cows eat bamboo in places where red pandas live. This leaves less bamboo for the red pandas. People hunt red pandas, too. They use the pandas' fur to make special good luck hats for newlyweds.

Red pandas are rare in the wild, but you can sometimes see them in zoos. These baby pandas were born at Australia's Taronga Zoo.

Helping the Red Panda

People are trying to save the few red pandas left in the wild. It is now against the law to kill them. Sadly, though, some people do not obey the law. People are also trying to teach farmers not to cut down the bamboo forests where red pandas live.

Today, there are several national parks where red pandas can live safely. For example, about 25 red pandas live in India's Singalila National Park. Zoos have been **breeding** red pandas and bringing them into parks like this one. Hopefully, this will help save the red panda.

Glossary

bamboo (bam-BOO) A thick, woody grass.

biscuits (BIS-kets) Small baked goods such as a roll.

breeding (BREED-ing) Bringing male and female animals together so they will have babies.

calories (KA-luh-reez) Amounts of food that the body uses to keep working.

energy (EH-nur-jee) The power to work or to act.

grunt (GRUNT) To make a short, deep sound.

mate (MAYT) To come together to make babies.

musk glands (MUSK GLANDZ) The parts of an animal's body that make and give off a strong smell.

patches (PACH-ez) Small places that are different from the place around them.

sole (SOHL) The bottom of a foot or shoe.

whistling (HWIH-suh-ling) Making a high, clear sound by blowing through the lips or teeth.

wrist (RIST) The place between the arm and the hand.

Index

B
bamboo, 4, 10, 12, 18, 20

C
China, 4

E
ears, 6, 18
eyes, 6, 18

F
face, 6, 12
false thumb, 8, 10
family, 4

forests, 4, 20, 22

I
India, 4

L
legs, 14

M
mountains, 4
musk glands, 16

N
Nepal, 4
nose, 6

P
patches, 6

R
raccoons, 6

S
sole, 8

T
tail, 6, 12, 16

Z
zoo(s), 10, 22

Web Sites

Due to the changing nature of Internet links, PowerKids Press has developed an online list of Web sites related to the subject of this book. This site is updated regularly. Please use this link to access the list:
www.powerkidslinks.com/paws/rpandas/